*Always
Near the Edge*

And for all this, nature is never spent;
There lives the dearest freshness deep down things;
And though the last lights off the black West went
Oh, morning, at the brown brink eastward, springs

— Gerard Manley Hopkins

Always Near the Edge

A Collection of Poetic Works

Richard A. Jansma

Foreword by
Linda Nemec Foster

Introduction by
Lauren K. Carlson

Edited by
Stanley Hagemeyer

HEART & LIFE
PUBLISHERS

Always Near the Edge
A Collection of Poetic Works
By Richard A. Jansma
AKA RAJ Conry

Edited by
Stanley Hagemeyer

© 2024 Stanley Hagemeyer
Heart & Life Publishers
Grand Rapids Michigan
ISBN: 9798218495343

The poems
"The Words," "Her Words," "Confessing," and
"One for the Ladies" appear in the chapbook
What Really Happened
© 1973 Richard Jansma
Pilot Press Books, Grand Rapids MI

CONTENTS

Foreword ~ Linda Nemec Foster   **11**

Introduction ~ Lauren K. Carlson   **15**

Divisions

    Sensuality   **21**

    Desolation   **37**

    Lyric   **71**

    Philosophical   **85**

    Hard Consolation   **93**

Biographic Sketch ~ Stanley Hagemeyer   **101**

About the Contributors   **107**

Foreword

Linda Nemec Foster
A Remembrance of Richard Jansma

I owe much of my life—my life as a poet, writer, literary presenter, and advocate for the arts—to Richard Jansma. As a matter of fact, Dick opened the door to the world of contemporary poetry and all its possibilities for me. I am forever grateful to him for his unwavering support and encouragement to a young woman he met in the fall of 1972.

In those autumn months, I lived in a house on Lake Drive in Grand Rapids near Aquinas College (my alma mater that I had recently graduated from in May of that year). I had received a degree in the social sciences—political science, sociology, and economics—and while I was working in that field as a social demographer at the Center for Environmental Study, I realized that my heart wasn't there. I was proficient in my job, but there was something else that called to me: a love of poetry. When I first read Dylan Thomas' brilliant poem, "Fern Hill," I knew what my life's passion was. I didn't major in English and took only one creative writing course at Aquinas from Herbert Woodward Martin, the amazing African-American professor and the college's poet-in-residence, but I knew what I loved.

Near my house was the Village Bookstore on Wealthy Street in the Eastown area. I would visit there often: looking at the shelves, paging through the many volumes of poetry that I couldn't afford, soaking in the ambience of a wonderful gathering place for people who loved books. It was at the Village

Bookstore that I heard about a poetry workshop the owners were hosting for the community. Free, no application guidelines, no previous publications or experience required. The only requirement: a desire to learn about poetry and share ideas. I immediately signed up.

And, it was at that first workshop I met other like-minded people who loved poetry. David Cope. Eric Greinke. And Richard Jansma. The workshop was small, never more than eight or ten people, and it would meet several times a month on a weekday evening. I had started writing very rough drafts (I wouldn't even call them poems) and would share that work with the group. While everyone was polite to this young and totally inexperienced writer, Dick Jansma took me aside after one session and said how much he admired what I was writing and what I was attempting to do on the page.

This support led to a mentorship and, later, a deep friendship. Dick introduced me to the poetry of so many great poets: from Whitman and Dickinson, to Ginsberg and Wakoski. It's not that I hadn't read or studied them before; it's just that Dick introduced me to the power of their language in a way I had never heard before. And, more importantly, he encouraged me to write my poems, to discover and celebrate my own voice. The voice of a granddaughter of immigrants from southern Poland. "Write what you know, Linda," he would often say to me. "But imagine what you can become."

When I got married in October of 1974 and moved to Detroit with my husband (Dick celebrated with us at our wedding in Cleveland), he strongly suggested I meet poet and artist Faye Kicknosway who was teaching at Wayne State University. "I heard her read at Ferris State University a few years ago and she's amazing. I know she can take you to the next level with your writing."

I did meet her. And, he was right. For several semesters, I took Kicknosway's classes at Wayne (evening classes that met twice a week from 7:00-9:00 pm) and learned about sestinas and villanelles, enjambment and line breaks, the importance of the words you put on the page and the silent blank space surrounding them. It was Faye Kicknosway who encouraged me as much as Dick Jansma did. In 1976, she told me about the first low residency MFA program for creative writing that Ellen Bryant Voigt had established at Goddard College in Vermont (this MFA program has subsequently moved to Warren Wilson College in North Carolina). She wrote a letter of recommendation for me and I was accepted in 1977.

From 1977-1979 I studied with such luminaries as Lisel Mueller, Stephen Dobyns, Donald Hall, Louise Gluck, Heather McHugh, Raymond Carver, Tobias Wolff, Ellen Bryant Voigt, and Robert Hass. A constellation of extraordinary poets and writers. At Goddard I honed my craft and my art: taking steps that began in those classes with Faye Kicknosway in Detroit, that began with those first poetry workshops with Richard Jansma in Grand Rapids.

Since then, I've continued to write and publish. My fourteenth collection of poetry will be published by Wayne State University Press in October of 2024. *Bone Country* and *The Blue Divide*, two of my most recent books, were nominated for the Pulitzer Prize in Poetry. In addition, my work has been honored with numerous Pushcart Prize nominations, three international awards from Ireland, a Michigan Notable Book Award, and first prize in the 2023 Allen Ginsberg Poetry Contest (Dick, you've got to be smiling at that). From 2003-2005, I was honored to serve as the inaugural Poet Laureate of Grand Rapids. A distinct honor that the young girl who met Richard Jansma in the fall of 1972 could never imagine. But he could.

My first collection of poetry, *A History of the Body*, was published by Coffee House Press of Minneapolis in September of 1987—soon after I came back to Grand Rapids with my family. Dick was overjoyed that we lived in the same city again. Two years before his death in December of 1989, I wrote this personal inscription to him on the title page of *A History of the Body:* "To Dick—For all your support, encouragement, and care. With much appreciation for your being there for me at the beginning of my writing. Much love, Linda Nemec Foster, 9/16/87."

When Dick died, he left me a large portion of his vast collection of books: poetry, novels, short stories, literary criticism. In a plastic bag, he had kept his copy of my first book. Pristine, clear, perfect. As if he wanted to say one last goodbye by reminding me that he was there at the very beginning of my long journey. I'll never forget.

Linda Nemec Foster
First Poet Laureate of Grand Rapids MI
Michigan Notable Book Author

Introduction

Lauren K. Carlson

Richard Jansma's poetry best exemplifies what St. John of the Cross refers to as the dark night of the soul. Similar to 'hard consolation' in Ignatian spirituality, the dark night is a way of describing God's inherent unknowability. Paradoxically, in the midst of this unknowing, God makes himself known. When an individual's capacity to endure ends, encounter with Spirit begins.

Unlike Linda and Stan, who knew Richard personally, my connection to Richard Jansma's poetry did not happen during his lifetime. Yet Richard, without knowing it, is partly responsible for my own career as a poet. I'd consider myself an emerging writer, someone at the beginning of what I hope will be a long and fruitful life of writing and reflection. Linda Nemec Foster, who has provided the foreword for this book, was once encouraged by Richard to keep writing, as Linda has encouraged me. I can't say where I'd be without this connection. It's been meaningful for Stan to bring us all together through this volume of Richard's work. I think Richard would be moved to know his legacy continues in ways he couldn't have predicted. I regret never knowing him but am thankful for the opportunity to encounter his work.

There are three poems in particular that I believe represent the best of Richard's work. They are, one: "I was always too young to die," two: "Confessing" (this is part of Richard's published chapbook *What Really Happened*), and finally three:

"Prayer the Night Before Surgery," also titled "Bloodsweat" in a prior draft.

Throughout Richard's work, several themes occupy the foreground of his writing. The categories represented have been used to order the collected volume of poetry. They are sensuality, desolation, the lyric, the philosophical, and hard consolation.

An excerpt from Richard's work may provide instruction and insight on how to best approach his poetry:

>   It is never the question
>   when is flesh   no longer
>   flesh
>   & words   the flawed melody
>   of our body
>   & flesh   our flesh
>   a coffin
>   for dreaming

Although not overtly present in this excerpt, Richard's illness looms in this passage. There's a sense of prodding, of questioning. When is flesh a coffin for dreaming? When is it otherwise? He writes "It is never the question" but what I see in the text is the opposite. Richard's questions are what bring him to the page. In this manuscript is a speaker who wrestles with his faith, but also someone whose faith buoys him against and alongside despair. Wretched is a word I sense Richard may have used to describe his emotional and physical toil. That this becomes a source of inspiration for creative output, to me, is evidence of transformation.

Richard seems to assert that in our flesh, our death (here denoted by the use of the word coffin) there is also a source of flourishing—"dreaming." There's a reference to the body, the carnal, the realm of the senses. Sensuality and suffering both were a substantial focus in Richard's work and a source of inspiration for his poetry.

While I get a sense of Richard's life from Stan's introduction and others that knew him, at times Richard's style focuses more on line breaks, unusual syntax, repetition, and spacing rather than narrative. The disjointed and formally inventive structures demonstrate active experimentation. I believe his work reflects interplay between song and story. In this collection there are longer elaborate poems juxtaposed with brief meditations, a characteristic typical of Jansma's writing.

Richard's work demonstrates as much philosophical reckoning as it does emotional catharsis. I believe his strongest poems happen when he is able to join the two. I hope that in ordering the poems, we've been able to show the full range of Richard's experience. The speaker here feels and thinks deeply. Suffering has impacted the speaker's life, but it doesn't comprise it.

I'll close with the observation that the phrase, "a coffin for dreaming" exemplifies one of the most moving elements of Richard's poetry, his work of hard consolation. Hard consolation is a phrase for understanding an abiding paradox of human life. Often when we find ourselves at our lowest and most desperate, that is when we may sense God's nearness. Believing the miracle of the incarnation can be known through real suffering—and a conviction that God made himself known through the passion of Christ, may transform the essence of our pain. This is why we've chosen to end the collected works with Richard's "Bloodsweat" followed by "I Am." It is through the suffering, through the coffin, that we arrive at our dreaming—a place of invitation.

In Stan's invitation to read Richard's work, I choose to see fingerprints of the divine. The circle of connection among Linda, Stan, Richard, and me, is a reminder of how each individual's life matters, and how our human creative work can hold more impact than we'll ever know.

Even if our life—or perhaps because life—is filled with suffering and despair, as Richard's poetry indicates his surely was, our faith, life, and work continue on. Engaging with Richard's work has been a great source of personal encouragement to me. In it, I see a model for genuine interrogation of faith through language. I also get a sense of that which is bigger than I am, a greater Thou who is at work doing far more than I could ask or imagine. For that, I'm truly grateful.

Lauren K. Carlson
July 1, 2024

Sensuality

I Was Always Too Young to Die

I was
always too young
to die
twenty-one
& wasting away
into white wet sheets

the hours marched on
on
needles & knives
codine
morphine
demerol
a fat white cat
purrs
softly
in the warm
sun

I dream
endlessly
of
brown eyes
brown thighs
coming
finally
into my own
LuAnn
the dream

never ends
I am
always
    almost
there
mirrored
in brown eyes
singing
in the warm
quicksilver moon

the charts
become memory
records
    of doctors
& days
        one
            by
      one

Self-Portrait

one of his eyes was like
a patch of brown grass
dropped carelessly in a
green field

the other, a glob of soft
fruit, warming itself on
a wooden table.

but when he placed himself
into canvas, with a wide selection
of pigments from which to choose,

he chose for his own eyes
a simple black, for he
had at that point gone beyond
the color to the sense.

The Words

I.
Oh   Suddenly
it is always   Saturday night
& her green eyes
                    hide
behind that maze
of mirrors
& a strange voice
            is saying
Do you want me
                  to go to bed
with you
sounding   oh sounding
that frozen field in
            the shadows of Nebraska
it is never the question
when is flesh   no longer
                  flesh
& words   the flawed melody
                of our body
& flesh   our flesh
               a coffin
for dreaming

II.
Do you want me to go to bed
with you   & how could I
when the words   Yes, those, just those
words
move me   bodily

      again to that 6th floor
where men   without eyes
gowned in green
listen
as the voices
again explain
we shall now begin
dissecting
& draw the silver scalpel

III.
Do you want me to   Do you want me to
Oh lost   on a sightless sea of green
can I live
if
seas of white cells
draw the life
from the withered roots of red cells
can I live
as flesh
      falls away
           from the bones
exposing
      an ancient
      apocalypse
can I live
if the voice
      is sucked
      away
by dark wind
can I live
as the eyes

are turned   inward on
decaying tissue
              inward on
bleached bones

IV.
There can be   no
waking
it will always be
Saturday night
& the echo bounces
bounces off the walls
of my skin
yes   oh yes
still
my blood
        turns black   black as
a Saturday night
                  in December
black as
the walls   my fingertips
cannot touch
& I know   I have no words
                for the question
was never asked
to bed with you   to bed with you

V.
Flesh is no longer
flesh
I have fallen

out of my skin
           into blackness
that engorges
                  a last scream
Do you want me   Do you want me

If You Were, But I Doubt That You Are:
For Richard Tiemersma

if you were walking through the quiet waves,
                        your smile would not be quite as hard
as it is now, resting on your head between
                        your hands. once you have suffered
death by water, then you will
                        suffer life. your face
will soften once again into the wings
                        of angels, softly brushing
against your eyes.
                        if your eyes entered heaven,
as your hands wish them to,
                        the order of your thoughts
would be disturbed
                        at their unaccustomed
freedom.

To The White Goddess
For Robert Graves

the hours   sands
     washed by the sea
even before the moon's
           birth
they have had their way
all I am   left with
     is a barren rock
   to cling to
while cold   angry claws
of the salt-
     heavy waters
   pull me down
into the hours
     & the restless
rhythm of a waiting moon

Prolegomena To Any Future Symbiotics

we were not born out of a mother's womb,
nor born, with blood, by glinting metal tools,
engendered not of spirits nor of ghouls,
nor resurrected into birth from tomb;

not rising from the dank and misty pools
like tadpoles leaving wet dark for the light,
no mother groaned, no father heaved for might
in sighings spent; not out of flesh of fools
and not with birth-stars burning in the night,
nor a charm to ensure the conception,
nor chants, nor prayers at the inception:
born out of seed not semen: only slight
but, gathering strength, awaited, thence, the birth,
when, parting rocks, we burst up out of the earth.

Sightings

Jesus walks the waters of Galilee
Moses' rod parts the Red Sea
Shadows of Eternity

Her Words
For S.K.

Her words that night
softly spoken
              floated before me
a knife   as she said
you must have   a lady
a lady   & of course, another
her slender fingers   two quiet doves
held like grappling hooks
while her eyes
                 blue
the blue of some early Grecian sea
as she said   I am
              your lady

The One Man Committee On Ways And Means

i suppose if the way it has to be is
this way, and if
i know no other way but
the way i am going, although I can see the others,
i will go the one way i am going
and nothing you can do can slow me down.

the sky is a blue skull with a dead light and a sun
for eyes. i can look it only
from the inside out, where the strain is,
lines of force and tension trying
to pull the system apart that will not come
apart. the creaks in the bone where
the hinges are is where i am, observing
the irregular set of points which defy
enumeration: getting up, walking, eating,
but there are so many more, that is why
the words cannot all be said that they are

i will make a beginning of naming the animals
in the beginning, the place to begin.

i will go the one way i am going,
and nothing you can do can slow me down.

Desolation

The First Time at Five or Swinging in the Rain

so you did it
did it & got caught
his momma saw you
& she's gonna tell
gonna get a whippin
for sure
when you get home
keep saying it
keep doing it
saying it
doing it
you're gonna get caught
Sister's gonna whack
your hand
good
with her ruler
a good whackin'
for doing it
& saying it
somebody's gonna tell
you did it   you did it
you did

Going Drinking With a Bunch of Degenerates

a cigarette on the floor, still smoking,
as you throw me the pen and i miss and have
to pick it up good lord the weed is stuck to
somebody's mouth. he is busy incinerating the
"do not remove under penalty of law" stickers from
the bottom of every chair with his mother-of-pearl
monogrammed butane throwaway lighter. this

poem is written on a fingernail,
for there is no other undestroyed surface.

if i wrote you a letter,
would you admit you were pregnant only an hour ago,
and seriously contemplating suicide?

if you were, would you die suffocated with gas, or
leap into the white that means the ground is frozen
under the bridge, or like i shall do, with
an angel beside me, waving with a poem
clutched in my hand addressed to no one in particular?

when my eyes go black
for the second time,
like the first time, when i caught
the fishhook in one, the sinker
in the other, only,
forever this time.

If You Care

If you care,
if you really care, Babe
don't pity me
Babe, don't pity me
jus' give me shelter
an' if you dig me,
if you really dig me, Babe
don't save me
oh Babe, don't save me
jus' give me shelter
Oh don' say nothin'
Babe, no talkin' at me
jus' quiet and gentle
an' if you touch my scars
with your slender fingers
jus' smile easylike, Babe
an' whisper yes in my ear
oh jus' let your fingers touch lightly
on my scars an' movin' on
softlike close my eyes
an' whisper what I need in my ears
an' cover my tears with your long blonde hair
Oh Babe, don' pity me, and don' save me
don' blame me an' don' shame me
jus' give me shelter
So be with me Babe, tonight
softlike an' easy
if you care
Babe, if you really care

Loving
for E.

Those hot summer nights
Naked on a scratchy wool blanket
A full moon bathing
Sweat   supple   steel
Of muscle   fire
Beneath the soft, golden moon
Of our flesh
We burned
Within   we   burned
Within each other
Those moments
& rose from our ashes
Like the harvest moon

Poem

The yellow light burns all through the black night;
Doggedly, I deny the spreading darkness its right.
In the flickering of shadows lurks what I fear:
A yelping pack of dogs – white of coat, red of ear.

Confessing

On our day
the sidewalk   blossomed
              into steam
the grass
      green & withering
as the people   fled
              the mushrooming concrete
Ann Arbor easily
        drained down
its spreading
        gutters
     into the stagnant Huron
And   on our day
where were we
Barbara   where were we
            sitting
locked
   into Angel Hall
staring at the walls
       during a bad hour
not listening
        to that man
with the steady drizzle
between his ears   & always
            that smile
In three hours
we were both   so mad
we even thought
thought   we might

                              go back
   to hell   hell
                              go back
   to the graduate
                    library to gather dust
   for empty hands

   You knew vaguely
             you were lost
                    very very lost
   & I could only try
   to listen   wondering
   when   my time would come
   My name is Barbara
                    not Carol
   you would tell me
          over & over again
   sitting in the shade
             counting your fingers
   saying   one's missing   one's missing
                              While I
   simply dreamt on
                    of my Carol
   so slim & sad
   prancing   across the stage
                    of my childhood

   On our day
   even the sun
             seemed exhausted
   your tired face   Barbara
                    with eyes
   like burnt-out forests

                 with deep lines
out of your mouth
                   was frightening
I could not look

So   on our day
as you wrung   your hands
                            into the night
trying   to stitch together
                 all the pieces
& tried   to talk
them to sleep

We were happy once
                 in Syracuse
we were both good Catholics
he taught school
& I stayed home
                 in a white house
with grass & trees all around
& went to night school

But   it wasn't enough
he had to get somewhere
after all
Syracuse was just a hick town
in a backwater area
of a failing state
he's traveling fast   now
the dissertation is nearly done
& he sleeps   to the hum
of an air conditioner
                       in a scarlet room

      punctually   every Tuesday
he invites me over
        to discuss the property settlement
            & the proper charges
to just wish me well
really   & to let me know
he's done the right thing
then   he turns off   the air conditioner
& the heat melts my dress
as he says
   this is Sharon
who has made me happy   at last
all I can see   in his eyes
are tiny sparks from
            her burning cunt
I can't find my way
           home

It was getting darker   Barbara
while your hands
        kept on trying
to feel
their way
that day
my cars   & eyes
were so tired
      still
your hands
      kept on
I was a good Catholic once
now I've broken every commandment
              but murder

I live
    in a house
with a man
who will not work
with a man
who will not live
with his wife
in the house
a house
with nine cats
three cactus plants
a cross
        some day
I will be burned
my ashes will be scattered
           over cactus plants

Barbara   Barbara
my head was nodding
        until
your drowning hands
           grabbed mine
&   you screamed
        out of the tree tops
Men Come Over and Fuck Me
like I was some cheap
            hole
in the wall bar
no one
    in my
          therapy group
will ever listen to me

just be a tree   Barbara
they say   just be a tree

So quiet   now
I could hear   crickets
along the Missouri
      rubbing the night
into ashes

            And her hands
in my hands
     still
I'll never go back
      to Syracuse
I don't even know
                where
it is   now

Her hands let go   at last
Barbara
I cannot see
a single thing
     except
the walls
I have been writing on
                it seems
forever
who can tell
where Syracuse is
I've never been there
but   Barbara

    if I find you
               again
    I'll listen
               better
    I really will
               listen

End-Place

the end of all things is the place
where the deer stop and drink,
where the water squeezes out
from the middle of the earth.

out of the middle of the earth,
where the hands that hold it together
are hit with a sharp spasm,
gracious lady, talking of poems
and glasses, how fine they are,
how carefully made, a leaf.

at this point the clear water turns
away in a crooked line to the sun,
through the rarefied, savage air,
breaking in pieces like ships off Carolina.

in the morning, when the air is crisp
as cold sheets, i will think of you.
i will turn into water where the wild dogs drink.
where they ask about the bees, where
they have gone.

when i become the water, first the bees
dip into me, and wet their wings, and
should have drowned, but carried me
away. the deer were thirsty, so the bees
turned into rain and washed their skins

and hooves, like lightning, hard as
stone.   the end of all things is the place
where water shivers together, clinging.

water and glasses like deer and dogs, drinking
water like eyeballs, the wave
of heat on the ocean we all participate
in making: the warmth you can see
of raindrops huddled together
in fear of dying, determined at the end
to make a last and desperate stand,

to turn into the stream before
we can be caught by the sun,
strung face up on the ground
and left to burn away.

before we are left to believe
all the lies that have been told us
we stand at the end-place, together,
our eyes like seeds in our hands.
we will plant them at once, like flowers,
they will grow and
in another body we will live
beyond the end-place, somewhere that is
warm, and very clear,
and as far as you can see.

The Cast

"I
am Nobody's
Fool
which is
the saddest part
of all."

The Future

The future?
All my plans
have
turned out
to be
for yesterday

Until the Next Goodbye
for Dee Modrowski

Wherever or whatever you are
or were or will be
you   blonde
braless in the bedroom
with lips and tongue
of the finest chamois
your gorgeous ass
and, oh, your hat!
where did you get it?
you
almost alone
can keep it all together
cunt and keenness
of mind
fast with the fifteen percent tip
good where and when it counts
practical enough to know
that we are all hung
on a question that has no answer
when the end finally comes
and you still in cocktail uniform
you will have a pure soul
in an unsavory world
for in this unsavory world
you have come to care
so may the angels greet you with B. B. King
may you dance on streets of gold
and may you taste the trinity like a ripe orange

and when the book of your life
is opened
may I be counted among the most necessary
words

Lonely days/Lonely nights

Give me the good old days when I would have someone to talk
to at this time of night someone who would talk to me talk
about the way the day had gone would go tomorrow and tomorrow
the days run on and I am alone feeling that time is the enemy
I will not be able to defeat defeat the drugs that I am long-
ing for for I long for drugs instead of a woman these days
these days drugs are the woman I love have unmanned me made
me the woman been made for so long so long that it doesn't
matter is what is the matter what is the matter is that I'm
alone in this night and the good old days were never that good
and I will die and know why I have to drive to Big Rapids to
get a book and see a friend a friend I had them then now they
now they are gone they have all gone into a circle of light
carried off to that greater world which we will never know
that we do not need because we have died done in by drugs that
we made love to to the drugs that we gave ourselves to to the
despair that drove us to the drugs to the drugs that drove
us to the despair in the air the error of thinking she would
love you all of your days she will love you all of your days
and she sleeps tonight with another man and I still feel what
the wise of this world the winners the wealthy feel they sleep
together in their money and their wisdom I sleep not at all never
have never will will never get any rest any rest for the wick-
ed time is the enemy time runs on faster than my fingers on
this machine do this not that do that not this don't do that
who could care now know who could care where there is no air
error of your love is fadin' fadin' and I'm gone

Saving Grace

Before a guy is very old he's got to learn
Not to over believe things.
Unless he's a guy like me.
If he's a guy like me he doesn't learn.

You find yourself after wrecks number
1, 2, and 3 still going down the same muddy road
Only you're farther down it and it's muddier,
In the first jalopy you ever owned.
And the springs are by this time
Absolutely ruined.   You say, Damn,
Damn, you say. If I'd had the money
I would have got rid of this thing,
I'd be on a good highway in some kind of sedan
All along knowing you had the money and you don't know where
It went but it's gone. So you're lying
To yourself and you know that too.

Thus knowing this and feeling greatly wise
You promise never to accuse your husband of smoking
Too much or buying a 50 dollar handsaw
When you can't even get 7 dollars together for groceries,
Like your mother did.   You look over,
To the seat beside you.   You see the husband
Isn't there.   What happened to him.
Well you ruined him in other ways.
So that's it. He didn't like the dents

You put in him.   So now he's got another woman.
So that's it.   So now he's got another woman
To put dents in him.

But maybe she won't.
Maybe she's perfect and they get along like peaches and cream.
And you will keep going along in the first jalopy you ever owned
Putting dents in one husband after another.

Only a guy's saving grace if you believe in one
Is to learn before he's very old not to over believe
In things.   Even in saving graces.

So maybe you won't put dents in another husband.
Maybe you will.
Maybe there won't be another husband.
Gee this jalopy aint that bad.
It aint that good neither.

One For The Ladies

If I could   thank you
for   those salty tears
that   smear your
mascara
& stain
your lovely breasts
But   as you know
I have decided
to be   a Jesuit
feeling   finally
that my hands   after all
these years
are the hands
            of a master
it would be better
            cleaner
 if I   were to wield
 the knife   myself

Monday Noon Mass

God and Jesus and the Holy Spirit
& Pam
with the big tits
when I was 35
& not tired from climbing steps
with three nurses watching
& me out of breath
& not 35
& Eric has written another experimental novel to
be rejected
when they bought the house
& me still not 35
holed up
on Thomas waiting
for the beginning
or the end
God, you follow any of this
experimental poem
Pam & Eric got a house
& surrealistic poetry
you can see through
but no big tits anymore
because you were never 35
& all your friends
suffer & die
every Monday at Mass

For My Grandfather Vander Ploeg

my grandfather:
they would not let you raise
cows in the big city,
but you somehow had to teach,
and there were no schools,
so you had to move to that city
if you were to raise anything at all.

three children had to grow,
so the cows of your dreams had to go,
had to go.

But they would not let your cows
in the big city. you
fooled them, grandfather.
they would let you build a barn,
so you did,
and though they would not by law allow
the raising of ruminants,
you fooled them, yes, you fooled them,
an elder telling folks you only
raised egg chickens, that your barn
was full of chickens that mooed.
and they had to believe you.

i can see you walking out this morning, seventeen years ago,
a pail for the liquid eggs your
chickens insisted on giving,
the four legged fools.

you fooled them, grandfather,
you fooled them.   and if
it weren't for the smell of manure,
you might have gotten away with it.

they took away your cows
and left you with chickens.
you couldn't grow cows forever, so
here am i.
here am i.

It Sure Did Rain A Lot

It sure did rain a lot that April. I
was too cold. Buses went too fast. Taxis
cost too much. All I could do was catch my
breath. That was it. Tops. That April the
girls were all too young. Or naive. Or too
old. Too experienced. Or just way too old.
They took my measure that April and found
me wanting. I was left with myself. Nothing
else. A narrow, malingering malcontent.
Sour on life, sour on love, sour on myself,
sour on the whole world. But for God's sake,
at least I made it. I survived. But it sure
did rain a lot that April.

Untitled

I suffer
therefore
I am
Why
therefore
am I

Untitled

Nothing is quite
as it ought to be

Cupboard doors standing open
Snow this morning, freezing rain
after the first true
spring day

Even the cat is restless:
Sometimes she mourns too & the ball of string
is just another ball of string

By tomorrow the front door will be repaired
The closets cleaned & empty
I will haul out the garbage
that begins to have something of an odor
pack up the stacks of dishes
get rid of the news from last evening's
paper: the grandmother next door has already
clipped out her favorite obituaries; I
would try the recipe with rice if I
had left
some pepper & rice

But we are clearing out the whole
house   we have lives we have to
get rid of

I do not understand it

Nothing is quite
as it ought to be

Day after tomorrow my husband is whisking me
off somewhere: Madison, Minneapolis, Moscow
It is still not clear
A decision will be made soon

I do not understand it
This old house has lots of room
I am only beginning to find my way
around here & you

oh I do not want to leave you
you are the one possible meaning
I have just begun to understand

I do not want to leave you

Where My Father And I Go For Walks

the route along the small road is a difficult
one, where we walk under the trees is a sacred place,
unique unto ourselves.
it is not our knees which bother us.
crawling through the warm grass,
the distance of our eyes from the object
alters our perception.
my father says
it's good to get away from things.
i think he is wrong,
i think the benefit of our position is that
we are once again able to get to the grass,
to experience each blade distinctly.
we seldom get a chance, father and i,
to see things so closely.

Apology by way of Prayer: Letter from Limbo

Dear God, I have over the years
trusted you in a cavalier fashion.
I have mouthed pieties and obeisances
While inwardly my heart raged with anger
Over my appointed lot.
Because you are God, I have expected
That my interests would necessarily be
Yours.
So I have expected you to stop the flow
of blood instead of rightly leaving me
To my just fate.   And in the chaos
Of diseased tissue and engulfing madness
I have expected your Word spoken in my behalf
To bring order. And so now, faced with the task
Of recouping the loss of wasted flesh and seeking
To bring discipline to spirit melancholy and mad,
I have searched the scriptures and mumbled prayers,
Seeking to win you by some petty magic
And thus, save myself from your fiercest gift.
But of course, it is not to be so;   You know
The spirit crying to be saved from itself.
So, now accept not a plea for forgiveness,
But a simple apology.   In fear and trembling
I take up my tools and accept my task.

At The End

Dear Marilyn,

never mind.

Lyric

2/23/75

I am sitting at my typewriter
again   I have spent nearly half the day
here   with birds and letters
and animals in foreign tongues outlandish costumes

and I have become
a lousy housekeeper
dishes undone   stove a mess
refrigerator all ice and a bit of an odor
crumbs on the floor without even a dog
and my husband out doing his own wash

and all the time I am thinking
of you   I
cannot bear your absence
even your absence to which
I have no legal right at all

tell me
may I keep it at least
your absence   with me here
by the typewriter
in the car when I
am alone

listen
if you have forgotten me
do not remember you left

your absence
here

I will keep it well
I promise you
I will hide it when
it needs protecting

please

do not call it out
in the cold

3/4/75

How can I say it
any other way

The sun is more fire than blood
today & I am leaping
into the hot white walls
of the sun's mouth
my own teeth are more gold than ivory
my lips more fruit than red
my heart a gay old celebration
my breasts two apples
& my eyes my eyes are each end
of a rainbow their many colors all one sea
so deep

My whole body open
like the fan of a peacock
glistening
just after rain

I fly to the top of your sails & we
represent every nation

I command the wind
I think I am more than a woman
might ever hope to be

look now my love
look now

you will never see
such
incredible
horizons
again

How Things Got Unmessed

She knew better right off, I was Prime beef, choice, pure corn
fed, Iowa's best. But I'd walked into a wall one too many times.
Come out pretty busted up, gutted, & ready for them green pastures,
& all the Alfalfa I could eat. But hell, she was definitely
the queen of any scene goin' down, could walk into any town &
right off, all the bad guys just lined up an' flew right. So
no way she couldn't handle what was left of Iowa's ex-main man.
From page one, we played the act her way, the way all the old
books read it. & ended flatout fucked. With most of my blood on
the basement floor. So she says, we need ourselves a cleaning
lady. An' so, the head cleanin' lady wiped up the blood and
what was left of my head. Then, she told the queen lookin' on,
he's mine now. And she put my head together so fine I could
whistle "Dixie." On Sunday. I could sing again, maybe not like
prime anymore. Still, pretty damned choice, honey, pretty choice.

Innocent Mind and Mayday in Girl and Boy

> And for all this, nature is never spent;
> There lives the dearest freshness
> deep down things;
> — *God's Grandeur*
> Gerard Manley Hopkins

Neither man nor woman   knows really
where a marriage begins
possibly in the first sharp interchange
of plowshare   and
the continually turning furrow
possibly in the coming together
of quiet April rains
and the black tumescent earth
possibly in the consummation
of the hot blaze of an August sun
and the spreading richness
of yellowing grain

No matter, no matter
wherever marriage begins
there is a harvest
and, once and again,
a poor yielding,
but any husbandman
of our mother   knows
"next year will be the year"
and takes heart

In this particular instance,
Stan and Mary Ann,

there is the Minnesota prairie
laced by cold northern winds
coming down from Canada—
winds fierce enough to freeze
a man and pick him clean
before sundown.
But every wind carries a new seed
new beginnings   a promise
of fertile green fields
to be tilled   a promise
of bounteous harvests
a sure promise of sustenance
for the hard winters ahead
bounteous enough to fulfill
our Mother Mary's wish:
"Growth in everything."
bounteous enough to gladden
the hearts of families, fish,
fowl, and flesh of all kind
bounteous enough to make a man and woman
dance and sing before the Lord
in thanksgiving.

And there is Michigan
with iron cities, acreages teeming
with Cherries, beans, potatoes,
the purple grape.
There is a daughter laughing
held in the embrace
of aunts and uncles, cousins, friends,
held close in the warmth
of a mother   the strength

of a father's workbred arms.
Out of this quiet warmth
this beautiful young girl
proves again God's unquenchable love
to love us.
A loving woman beautiful
as the fresh, gentle daisies,
as the happy songs and smells
of a family kitchen;
a young woman beautiful—
glorious, not just in what she
does, but what she is:
a fresh Eden
in the heart of her husband.

Beginnings, children, marriages,
we cannot know the time of beginnings,
when this marriage began.　　Still, we praise
and thank our God
for guarding the greatly blossoming
of the fragile seedling,
thank Him for guarding
each petal of each daisy,
even thank those dark gods
of lost withered plants.

Neither man nor woman
knows　　really
where a marriage begins
but we see here, in Stan and Mary Ann,
a particular redeeming instance.

7/30/79

Advent Song

words falling from the sky
to snow glazed ground
the riddle of love cannot say why
yet they fall silently
with heavenly sound–
mother's lullaby sung ever so softly

Song

Can I write a song of ten syllables
Which will say more than that I die daily
In search of a craft that will free me from
The terror of knowing myself dying?

Untitled

All day I wait,
silent upon a couch,
bathed by the pale autumn sun,
surrounded by suns
and memories of the moon
which for so many years
possessed me.
All night I wait
for the orange
of the harvest moon
to come to me in darkness,
to touch my lips
softly, softly,
to gently caress my loins.
So each day and each night
I wait,   wait
for you to come back.
Now my soul, the moon,
cannot cast even reflected light,
for I am alone on my couch,
dying under the sun's harsh glare.
Slowly, ever more slowly, the breath
passes between my lips.
Death will come at high noon
for I am a prisoner of the sun
and cannot any longer
call back
my moon, my love, my life.

Philosophical

Hurry please it's time
With thanks to Messrs. Jagger, Eliot, Bolan, et al

Hurry please it's time
If ah don't get some
shelter ah know ah'm goin' to fade away
But always at my back I hear
time's winged chariot hurrying near
Oh babe, it's just a kiss away
It's just a shot away
The grave's a fine and private place
but none do therein I think embrace

Hurry up please it's time
You slide so good
With bones so fair
You've got the universe
reclining in your hair
tryin' to make her connection
a kiss away, a shot away
and when ah'm sad
ah slide
a shot away

Hurry please it's time
I said how can I *lay*
When all I do is *play*

Untitled

My tears hang
Like drunken bats
In the dark cave
of my skull
the cold whistle
of blue shadows
dances through my lost cells
each bearing a single syllable
each a tear   I cannot speak
a tablet unrolls
You Are Dying
the blank page says
Dying   dying of what
of a world lost
lost
before I knew
it existed
the sun reeks
like an old boat
the moon has no glory   to mirror
& I have no glory
In my empty bed
   my   hands cannot hold
on to those
who could save me
For I will not be saved
having lost
more than half
my years

more tears than my life can
understand

God   let me love
even the littlest thing
let me know   a life
outside this black cave
let me know   a light
in this cave
let me find   one thing
that needs my light

Alone in this dark cave
I cannot even cast
a shadow
at the sun's midtide

Study In Black And White, For David

The night is as black
as Auden's eyes used to be, before he grew grey,
reading in old books.

I would not like that fate for you, beloved.
You ought to remain young forever,
and your eyes ought always to be black.
You can do that if you do now what I tell you,
I found this, after my eyes had faded blind
reading in a strange old book.

Get up to see the sunrise, return to sleep,
Awake to see the sunset, then to sleep again.
Your life will be one of infinitely great beginnings,
And there must be only beginnings.
Your body will not know it has lived a day,
and what it does not know
can't hurt it.

What is white is indefinite,
What is white like snow will melt in time.
What is black is always black.   Now,
while your eyes are yet so dark
Do not let them learn what a day will do to them,
But open them only
twice a day, and do not count the times
you work the lids.

What is white like snow will melt in time
But what is black will always be black: witness the night:

This night like every other night is black as any other black
Keep your eyes black, beloved,
As long as what you see is black
There can be no damnation.
As long as what you see is black
There still is hope for resurrection.

Hard Consolation

Bloodsweat or
Prayer the Night Before Surgery

Bloodsweat sucks breath
down the chest, pelvis,
out the toes
pink toenails
on gold carpet.
Gasp with fierceness
the thrust of knife
into gut.
Fight, breathe, fight
the fever, the raw
scraping pain.
Wires & tubes
blossom
from the bed.
Blood, tetracycline
follow gravity's
law & no other.
Telephone cords
stitch
friends & doctors
to bloodsweat.
Pain begins
the ruthless
search of the waters
of body & soul.
A thought is

a scream.
Memory is the melody
of knives scouring
the raw wound.

Come, gentle Jesus
nailed
to a wooden cross.
Be with me,
Jesus, in my agony.
Console the teeming
cities of my soul.
Let the sword
that pierced
your side
be with the pain
in a dark room.
"Bruised, divided, full of pain", [1]
You suffered
life and death
that I
in all this
might live.

Make my suffering
part
of your Passion.
Transform all agony
into Calvary.
Jesus, gentle brother,
bold with blood,
hear my cry,

my scream, take me
in your strong arms,
carpenter's arms,
teach me,
even in bloodsweat,
to know the joy
of Calvary.

                      1. Mother Teresa of Calcutta:
                          Something Beautiful For God

I Am

I am song
will you sing me?

I am question
will you ask me?

I am silence
will you hear me?

I am emptiness
will you fill me?

I am darkness
will you find a way in me?

I am a cry
will you utter me?

I am pain
will you embrace me?

If this be true
will you?

Biographical Sketch

Stanley Hagemeyer

My friend, Richard, always too young to die, passed away on December 11, 1989. He had entrusted me with keeping his papers and distributing his books to people and libraries he loved. His apartment was crowded with books, so the task was challenging. Near the end of that work I was stymied with what to do with three volumes on literary criticism. I made an appointment to offer them to our daughter's high school English teacher. She had empowered our daughter to become a confident creative writer. When I visited that teacher, I had a big surprise.

As she opened the first book and saw Richard's name inside, she asked, with a slight tremor, "Did these books really belong to Richard Jansma?" She seemed awed, as if he were a famous person. I assured her they had belonged to him. She went on to tell me she attended a creative writing course he taught as a graduate student instructor. "He was the best teacher I ever had!" Her testimony illustrated what was lost in Richard's shortened life, but also how his gifts blessed an unknown number in later generations. He had continued to encourage young writers like herself during his later decades, unemployed, but always engaged. Linda Nemec Foster's Foreword gives her own testimony to Richard Jansma's influence.

Richard was born in 1936 in northwest Iowa. As a vigorous boy, he enjoyed play and study. Following the death of his mother, Pearl Conry Jansma in 1946, his father remarried. Richard was a brilliant student and athlete, especially enjoying football, but at sixteen he developed severe colitis and soon experienced his first surgery. Perhaps his grief at losing his mother persisted and nurtured his illness. Effective treatment for the disorder was not yet common as in later decades. The disease became a permanent part of his life and later developed into ileitis. However, in spite of his illness, he successfully attended Northwestern College in Orange City, IA and later Hope College in Holland, MI, graduating in 1961. Always a brilliant student, he persisted in spite of frequent visits to hospitals and occasional surgeries. Friends in college noticed he never studied for tests. He was usually found reading a novel while others crammed. Yet he consistently emerged with top grades. Whatever he read always seemed to stick in his mind, he once told me.

Upon graduation he married his longtime college girl friend. Several of his closest friends were planning to attend Western Theological Seminary in Holland the next year. He also chose to study there one year before transferring to Michigan State University. Later, he informed me he only attended the seminary that year because he wanted to read Paul Tillich's theological works. At Michigan State he intended to complete a Ph.D. in English Literature. During his first years there he did well, continued to write his own poetry and taught English, short story, poetry, and creative writing as a graduate student instructor. He also commuted to teach at Central Michigan University for two years.

However, his health continued to plague him, and further hospitalizations occurred. When I visited them in 1968 he was as delightful a conversationalist as ever. But his marriage was eroding. Not long after that, his wife filed for divorce and married a fellow student whom Richard had considered to be one of his best friends.

That devastating experience drove Richard's physical and emotional health into a downward spiral. Eventually the department head asked him to give up on the Ph.D. and accept an M.A. based on work he had completed. Following that disappointment, he spent a year pursuing a Master's degree in library science at the University of Michigan. However, his irregular health caused periodic stays in hospitals and interrupted his progress.

Finally, in desperation, he gave up his studies and moved to Grand Rapids where a friend from his college years was teaching at Calvin College. Richard had the impression this friend would help him find a teaching position in the area. However, after moving, he discovered this friend had little time or interest in promoting Richard's career. This disappointment sent him spiraling further into depression and agonizing episodes of his illness. For a few months he held a job as a janitor at a grade school, but then was released when he needed to be hospitalized. Again in desperation, he applied for disability support.

In spite of this cavalcade of frustrations, he continued to make acquaintances at poetry readings and gained respect in the circles of local and regional literati. He took part in judging events and did readings at notable gatherings. However, he became addicted to pain medications and endured many long and lonely sleepless nights. One of his best seasons developed through the help of a few Catholic friends who persistently cared for him through his rough times. Their attention eventually led him to take instruction through the Catholic Information Center. He felt he was returning to the church of his mother, who had been Catholic. In his copy of *The New Catechism* he wrote his name and "Born again November 15, 1974."

For a while things seemed to get better. He began to paint as well as write, and he continued to buy books which he read voraciously. Eventually, his car was broken into and vandalized. Following that loss, he never again owned a vehicle. Fortunately, he found a subsidized apartment in downtown Grand Rapids not far from the library he loved.

In the late 1970s he broke a hip due to osteoporosis caused by the frequent use of steroids prescribed to control the inflammation in his gut. Later, after extensive surgery to reorient his legs for more stability, he spent three weeks in our home for recovery.

During his extended stays in the hospital he often asked me to bring three or four books from his apartment. By this time, there were thousands of books on shelves surrounding his living area, plus tiers on every wall in the bedroom and even in his closet. But he easily directed me to each book's location, such as "the east wall, second shelf, about the tenth book from the left end." He seemed to know every volume's position. Our frequent conversations ranged from politics to art history, literature, and sports. He easily called to mind the world series champions of each year for decades. He became a part of our family and was in our home often for birthdays or holidays.

Eventually he decided that since he couldn't get a job, but knew that he had significant gifts to offer, perhaps he could join a Catholic religious order. After researching carefully which order might suit him, he applied. An interview was arranged and seemed to go very well. However, after several weeks of waiting, he received a letter informing him that although he had much to offer, the order could not accept responsibility for his chronic health problems, and must therefore decline his application. Following that disappointment his health conditions increasingly wore him down. He felt hopeless, and frequently argued his case with God, once telling me "I don't know anymore if there is a God, but if there is, he doesn't like me."

When Richard died we held a service at the Paulist Center in Grand Rapids, attended by about twenty-five friends. It was the end of Richard's long journey of only fifty-three years. His writing reflects the pain of that journey, but also the depths of life he understood and celebrated. I am pleased to share some of his works in this volume with old friends and a new generation of readers.

Stanley Hagemeyer

Contributors

Linda Nemec Foster has published fourteen collections of poetry, including *The Lake Huron Mermaid, Bone Country, The Blue Divide, Amber Necklace from Gdansk*, and *The Lake Michigan Mermaid* (2019 Michigan Notable Book), which was created with co-author Anne-Marie Oomen and artist Meridith Ridl. Her work appears in magazines and journals such as *The Georgia Review, Nimrod, New American Writing, North American Review, Witness, Verse Daily*, and the *Best Small Fictions Anthology 2022*. She has received nominations for the Pulitzer Prize and Pushcart Prize and awards from the Arts Foundation of Michigan, National Writer's Voice, Dyer-Ives Foundation, The Poetry Center (NJ), *Fish Anthology* (Ireland), and the Academy of American Poets. The first Poet Laureate of Grand Rapids, Michigan (2003-2005, Foster is the founder of the Contemporary Writers Series at Aquinas College. For more information see lindanemecfoster.com

Lauren K. Carlson is a poet and spiritual director living in Manistee, Michigan. Her work has recently appeared in *Crab Creek Review, Salamander Magazine, Terrain, The Windhover* and *Waxwing*. In 2022 she won the Levis Stipend from Friends of Writers for her manuscript in progress. Her writing has been supported by Tin House, Napa Valley Writers' Conference and Sewanee Writers' Conference. She currently serves as editor for *Tinderbox Poetry Journal* and holds an MFA in poetry from the Warren Wilson MFA Program for Writers. For more information see laurenkcarlson.com.

Stanley Hagemeyer writes short stories and historical fiction. His recent story "Eye Witness" was published in *Making Waves 2024*. He has served as a senior pastor, an interim professor of pastoral care, and interim pastor for several churches in transition. Earlier, as founder of The Good News Community in Grand Rapids, Michigan, he led a ministry serving hundreds of newly divorced individuals and trained many of them to conduct peer support groups. During that time, he co-authored *Ministry to the Divorced*. More recently he has trained care teams for churches. His book *Courage to Care: You Can Help Others Who Are Suffering* offers similar help. He continues to coach several professionals in ministry. Living on a quiet lake in the woods near Ludington, Michigan, he and his wife enjoy the respite of the natural world daily.

www.ingramcontent.com/pod-product-compliance
Lightning Source LLC
LaVergne TN
LVHW092054060526
838201LV00047B/1392